Weekly Planner 2020

Car Collector

Name:

_____

_____

Model Name _____

Collector Number _____ Brand _____

Year _____ Series _____ Wheel Type _____

Country _____ Designer _____

Colors

Overall Color Scheme _____

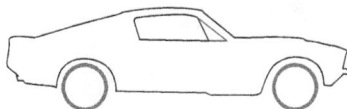

Base _____ Window _____

Fender _____ Interior _____

Notes

Where bought? _____

Date Acquired _____

Condition _____

December

Week 1   12/30/19 - 01/05/20

○ 30. MONDAY

PRIORITIES

○ 31. TUESDAY

○ 1. WEDNESDAY

TO DO

○ 2. THURSDAY

○ 3. FRIDAY

○ 4. SATURDAY / 5. SUNDAY

Model Name _____

Collector Number _____   Brand _____

Details

Year _____   Series _____   Wheel Type _____

Country _____   Designer _____

Colors

Overall Color Scheme _____

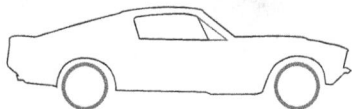

Base _____   Window _____

Fender _____   Interior _____

Where bought? _____

Date Acquired _____

Condition _____

Notes

_____

_____

_____

_____

_____

January

Week 2   01/06/20 - 01/12/20

○ 6. MONDAY

PRIORITIES

○ 7. TUESDAY

○ 8. WEDNESDAY

TO DO

○ 9. THURSDAY

○ 10. FRIDAY

○ 11. SATURDAY / 12. SUNDAY

Model Name _____

Collector Number _____ Brand _____

Details

Year _____ Series _____ Wheel Type _____

Country _____ Designer _____

Colors

Overall Color Scheme _____

Base _____ Window _____

Fender _____ Interior _____

Where bought? _____

Date Acquired _____

Condition _____

Notes

_____

_____

_____

_____

_____

January

01/13/20 - 01/19/20

○ 13. MONDAY

PRIORITIES

○ 14. TUESDAY

○ 15. WEDNESDAY

TO DO

○ 16. THURSDAY

○ 17. FRIDAY

○ 18. SATURDAY / 19. SUNDAY

Model Name

_____

Collector Number _____ Brand _____

Year _____ Series _____ Wheel Type _____

Country _____ Designer _____

— Colors —

Overall Color Scheme _____

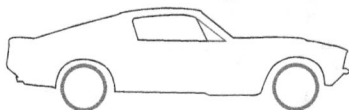

Base _____ Window _____

Fender _____ Interior _____

Where bought? _____

Date Acquired _____

Condition _____

— Notes —

_____

_____

_____

_____

_____

January

Week 4   01/20/20 - 01/26/20

○ 20. MONDAY

                                          PRIORITIES
                                          _____
                                          _____
_____   _____

○ 21. TUESDAY   _____
                                          _____
                                          _____
                                          _____
_____   _____

○ 22. WEDNESDAY

                                          TO DO
                                          _____
_____   _____

○ 23. THURSDAY   _____
                                          _____
                                          _____
                                          _____
_____   _____

○ 24. FRIDAY   _____
                                          _____
                                          _____
                                          _____
_____   _____

○ 25. SATURDAY / 26. SUNDAY   _____
                                          _____
                                          _____
_____   _____

Model Name

Collector Number _____   Brand _____

Details

Year _____   Series _____   Wheel Type _____

Country _____   Designer _____

Colors

Overall Color Scheme _____

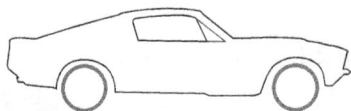

Base _____   Window _____

Fender _____   Interior _____

Where bought? _____

Date Acquired _____

Condition _____

Notes

_____

_____

_____

_____

_____

January

01/27/20 - 02/02/20

○ 27. MONDAY

PRIORITIES

○ 28. TUESDAY

○ 29. WEDNESDAY

TO DO

○ 30. THURSDAY

○ 31. FRIDAY

○ 1. SATURDAY / 2. SUNDAY

Model Name _____

Collector Number _____ Brand _____

Details

Year _____ Series _____ Wheel Type _____

Country _____ Designer _____

Colors

Overall Color Scheme _____

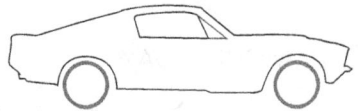

Base _____ Window _____

Fender _____ Interior _____

Where bought? _____

Date Acquired _____

Condition _____

Notes

_____

_____

_____

_____

_____

_____

February

02/03/20 - 02/09/20

○ 3. MONDAY

PRIORITIES

○ 4. TUESDAY

○ 5. WEDNESDAY

TO DO

○ 6. THURSDAY

○ 7. FRIDAY

○ 8. SATURDAY / 9. SUNDAY

Model Name

_____

Collector Number _____   Brand _____

Details

Year _____   Series _____   Wheel Type _____

Country _____   Designer _____

Colors

Overall Color Scheme _____

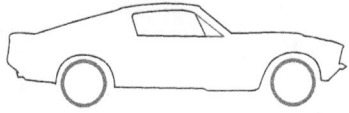

Base _____   Window _____

Fender _____   Interior _____

Notes

Where bought? _____

Date Acquired _____

Condition _____

February

Week 7   02/10/20 - 02/16/20

○ 10. MONDAY

○ 11. TUESDAY

○ 12. WEDNESDAY

TO DO

○ 13. THURSDAY

○ 14. FRIDAY

○ 15. SATURDAY / 16. SUNDAY

Model Name

_____

Collector Number _____ Brand _____

Details

Year _____ Series _____ Wheel Type _____

Country _____ Designer _____

Colors

Overall Color Scheme _____

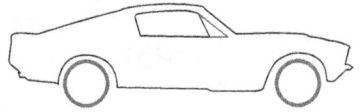

Base _____ Window _____

Fender _____ Interior _____

Where bought? _____

Date Acquired _____

Condition _____

Notes

_____

_____

_____

_____

_____

February

○ 17. MONDAY

PRIORITIES

○ 18. TUESDAY

○ 19. WEDNESDAY

TO DO

○ 20. THURSDAY

○ 21. FRIDAY

○ 22. SATURDAY / 23. SUNDAY

Model Name

_____

Collector Number _____ Brand _____

Details

Year _____ Series _____ Wheel Type _____

Country _____ Designer _____

Colors

Overall Color Scheme _____

Base _____ Window _____

Fender _____ Interior _____

Where bought? _____

Date Acquired _____

Condition _____

Notes

_____

_____

_____

_____

_____

_____

February

02/24/20 - 03/01/20

○ 24. MONDAY

PRIORITIES

○ 25. TUESDAY

○ 26. WEDNESDAY

TO DO

○ 27. THURSDAY

○ 28. FRIDAY

○ 29. SATURDAY / 1. SUNDAY

Model Name

Collector Number _____ Brand _____

┌─ **Details** ──┐

Year _____ Series _____ Wheel Type _____

Country _____ Designer _____

└──┘

┌─ **Colors** ───┐

Overall Color Scheme _____

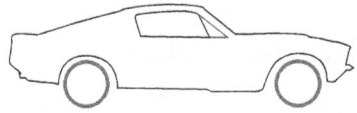

Base _____ Window _____

Fender _____ Interior _____

└──┘

Where bought? _____

Date Acquired _____

Condition _____

┌─ **Notes** ────────────────────┐

_____

_____

_____

_____

_____

└──────────────────────────────┘

March

03/02/20 - 03/08/20

○ 2. MONDAY

PRIORITIES

○ 3. TUESDAY

○ 4. WEDNESDAY

TO DO

○ 5. THURSDAY

○ 6. FRIDAY

○ 7. SATURDAY / 8. SUNDAY

Model Name

_____

Collector Number _____ Brand _____

Details

Year _____ Series _____ Wheel Type _____

Country _____ Designer _____

Colors

Overall Color Scheme _____

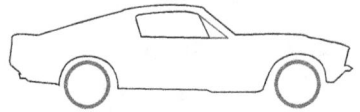

Base _____ Window _____

Fender _____ Interior _____

Where bought? _____

Date Acquired _____

Condition _____

Notes

_____

_____

_____

_____

_____

March

○ 9. MONDAY

PRIORITIES

○ 10. TUESDAY

○ 11. WEDNESDAY

TO DO

○ 12. THURSDAY

○ 13. FRIDAY

○ 14. SATURDAY / 15. SUNDAY

Model Name _____

Collector Number _____ Brand _____

Details

Year _____ Series _____ Wheel Type _____

Country _____ Designer _____

Colors

Overall Color Scheme _____

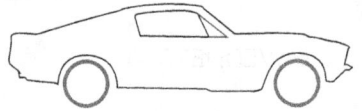

Base _____ Window _____

Fender _____ Interior _____

Notes

Where bought? _____

Date Acquired _____

Condition _____

March

Week 12

○ 16. MONDAY

PRIORITIES

○ 17. TUESDAY

○ 18. WEDNESDAY

TO DO

○ 19. THURSDAY

○ 20. FRIDAY

○ 21. SATURDAY / 22. SUNDAY

Model Name _____

Collector Number _____   Brand _____

Details

Year _____   Series _____   Wheel Type _____

Country _____   Designer _____

Colors

Overall Color Scheme _____

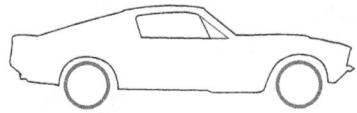

Base _____   Window _____

Fender _____   Interior _____

Notes

Where bought? _____   _____

Date Acquired _____   _____

                                  _____

Condition _____   _____

                              _____

March

03/23/20 - 03/29/20

○ 23. MONDAY

PRIORITIES

_____

○ 24. TUESDAY

_____

○ 25. WEDNESDAY

TO DO

_____

○ 26. THURSDAY

_____

○ 27. FRIDAY

_____

○ 28. SATURDAY / 29. SUNDAY

_____

Model Name _____

Collector Number _____ Brand _____

— **Details** ———————————————————

Year _____ Series _____ Wheel Type _____

Country _____ Designer _____

— **Colors** ———————————————————

Overall Color Scheme _____

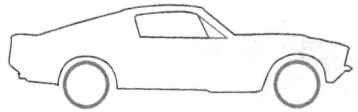

Base _____ Window _____

Fender _____ Interior _____

Where bought? _____

Date Acquired _____

Condition _____

— **Notes** ———————————————————

_____

_____

_____

_____

_____

March

Week 14   03/30/20 - 04/05/20

○ 30. MONDAY

PRIORITIES

_____

○ 31. TUESDAY

_____

_____

_____

_____

○ 1. WEDNESDAY

TO DO

_____

○ 2. THURSDAY

_____

_____

_____

_____

○ 3. FRIDAY

_____

_____

_____

_____

○ 4. SATURDAY / 5. SUNDAY

_____

_____

_____

Model Name _____

Collector Number _____   Brand _____

Details

Year _____   Series _____   Wheel Type _____

Country _____   Designer _____

Colors

Overall Color Scheme _____

Base _____   Window _____

Fender _____   Interior _____

Where bought? _____

Date Acquired _____

Condition _____

Notes

_____

_____

_____

_____

_____

_____

April

Week 15

04/06/20 - 04/12/20

○ 6. MONDAY

PRIORITIES

○ 7. TUESDAY

○ 8. WEDNESDAY

TO DO

○ 9. THURSDAY

○ 10. FRIDAY

○ 11. SATURDAY / 12. SUNDAY

Model Name _____

Collector Number _____   Brand _____

Details

Year _____   Series _____   Wheel Type _____

Country _____   Designer _____

Colors

Overall Color Scheme _____

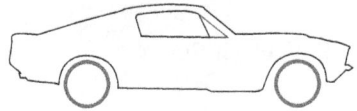

Base _____   Window _____

Fender _____   Interior _____

Notes

Where bought? _____

Date Acquired _____

Condition _____

_____
_____
_____
_____
_____

April

Week 16

04/13/20 - 04/19/20

○ 13. MONDAY

PRIORITIES

○ 14. TUESDAY

○ 15. WEDNESDAY

TO DO

○ 16. THURSDAY

○ 17. FRIDAY

○ 18. SATURDAY / 19. SUNDAY

Model Name _____

Collector Number _____ Brand _____

Details

Year _____ Series _____ Wheel Type _____

Country _____ Designer _____

Colors

Overall Color Scheme _____

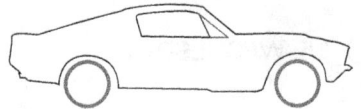

Base _____ Window _____

Fender _____ Interior _____

Notes

Where bought? _____

Date Acquired _____

Condition _____

April

Week 17

04/20/20 - 04/26/20

○ 20. MONDAY

PRIORITIES

○ 21. TUESDAY

○ 22. WEDNESDAY

TO DO

○ 23. THURSDAY

○ 24. FRIDAY

○ 25. SATURDAY / 26. SUNDAY

Model Name

Collector Number _____   Brand _____

Details

Year _____   Series _____   Wheel Type _____

Country _____   Designer _____

Colors

Overall Color Scheme _____

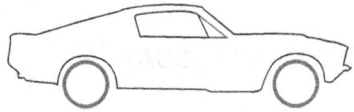

Base _____   Window _____

Fender _____   Interior _____

Notes

Where bought? _____

Date Acquired _____

Condition _____

April

04/27/20 - 05/03/20

○ 27. MONDAY

PRIORITIES

○ 28. TUESDAY

○ 29. WEDNESDAY

TO DO

○ 30. THURSDAY

○ 1. FRIDAY

○ 2. SATURDAY / 3. SUNDAY

Model Name

_____

Collector Number _____ Brand _____

Details

Year _____ Series _____ Wheel Type _____

Country _____ Designer _____

Colors

Overall Color Scheme _____

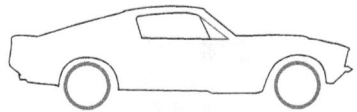

Base _____ Window _____

Fender _____ Interior _____

Notes

Where bought? _____

Date Acquired _____

Condition _____

May

Week 19

05/04/20 - 05/10/20

○ 4. MONDAY

PRIORITIES

○ 5. TUESDAY

○ 6. WEDNESDAY

TO DO

○ 7. THURSDAY

○ 8. FRIDAY

○ 9. SATURDAY / 10. SUNDAY

Model Name

Collector Number _____ Brand _____

Details

Year _____ Series _____ Wheel Type _____

Country _____ Designer _____

Colors

Overall Color Scheme _____

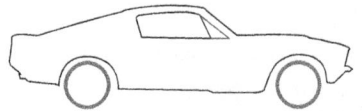

Base _____ Window _____

Fender _____ Interior _____

Where bought? _____

Date Acquired _____

Condition _____

Notes

_____

_____

_____

_____

_____

May

05/11/20 - 05/17/20

○ 11. MONDAY

PRIORITIES

_____

_____

○ 12. TUESDAY

_____

_____

_____

_____

○ 13. WEDNESDAY

TO DO

_____

_____

○ 14. THURSDAY

_____

_____

_____

_____

○ 15. FRIDAY

_____

_____

_____

_____

○ 16. SATURDAY / 17. SUNDAY

_____

_____

_____

Model Name _____

Collector Number _____ Brand _____

Details

Year _____ Series _____ Wheel Type _____

Country _____ Designer _____

Colors

Overall Color Scheme _____

Base _____ Window _____

Fender _____ Interior _____

Where bought? _____

Date Acquired _____

Condition _____

Notes

_____

_____

_____

_____

_____

May

Week 21

05/18/20 - 05/24/20

○ 18. MONDAY

PRIORITIES

○ 19. TUESDAY

○ 20. WEDNESDAY

TO DO

○ 21. THURSDAY

○ 22. FRIDAY

○ 23. SATURDAY / 24. SUNDAY

Model Name

Collector Number _____   Brand _____

Details

Year _____   Series _____   Wheel Type _____

Country _____   Designer _____

Colors

Overall Color Scheme _____

Base _____   Window _____

Fender _____   Interior _____

Notes

Where bought? _____

Date Acquired _____

Condition _____

May

Week 22

○ 25. MONDAY

PRIORITIES

○ 26. TUESDAY

○ 27. WEDNESDAY

TO DO

○ 28. THURSDAY

○ 29. FRIDAY

○ 30. SATURDAY / 31. SUNDAY

Model Name _____

Collector Number _____ Brand _____

Details

Year _____ Series _____ Wheel Type _____

Country _____ Designer _____

Colors

Overall Color Scheme _____

Base _____ Window _____

Fender _____ Interior _____

Notes

Where bought? _____ _____

Date Acquired _____ _____

_____

Condition _____ _____

_____

_____

June

Week 23   06/01/20 - 06/07/20

○ 1. MONDAY

PRIORITIES

_____

_____

○ 2. TUESDAY

_____

_____

_____

_____

○ 3. WEDNESDAY

TO DO

_____

_____

○ 4. THURSDAY

_____

_____

_____

_____

○ 5. FRIDAY

_____

_____

_____

_____

○ 6. SATURDAY / 7. SUNDAY

_____

_____

_____

Model Name

Collector Number _____   Brand _____

Details

Year _____   Series _____   Wheel Type _____

Country _____   Designer _____

Colors

Overall Color Scheme _____

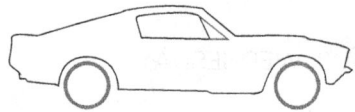

Base _____   Window _____

Fender _____   Interior _____

Notes

Where bought? _____

Date Acquired _____

Condition _____

June

06/08/20 - 06/14/20

○ 8. MONDAY

PRIORITIES

○ 9. TUESDAY

○ 10. WEDNESDAY

TO DO

○ 11. THURSDAY

○ 12. FRIDAY

○ 13. SATURDAY / 14. SUNDAY

Model Name _____

Collector Number _____ Brand _____

Details

Year _____ Series _____ Wheel Type _____

Country _____ Designer _____

Colors

Overall Color Scheme _____

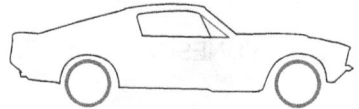

Base _____ Window _____

Fender _____ Interior _____

Where bought? _____

Date Acquired _____

Condition _____

Notes

_____

_____

_____

_____

_____

June

Week 25   06/15/20 - 06/21/20

○ 15. MONDAY

PRIORITIES

○ 16. TUESDAY

○ 17. WEDNESDAY

TO DO

○ 18. THURSDAY

○ 19. FRIDAY

○ 20. SATURDAY / 21. SUNDAY

Model Name _____

Collector Number _____   Brand _____

Details

Year _____   Series _____   Wheel Type _____

Country _____   Designer _____

Colors

Overall Color Scheme _____

Base _____   Window _____

Fender _____   Interior _____

Where bought? _____

Date Acquired _____

Condition _____

Notes

_____

_____

_____

_____

_____

_____

June

06/22/20 - 06/28/20

○ 22. MONDAY

PRIORITIES

_____

_____

○ 23. TUESDAY

_____

_____

_____

_____

○ 24. WEDNESDAY

TO DO

_____

_____

○ 25. THURSDAY

_____

_____

_____

_____

○ 26. FRIDAY

_____

_____

_____

_____

○ 27. SATURDAY / 28. SUNDAY

_____

_____

_____

Model Name _____

Collector Number _____ Brand _____

Details

Year _____ Series _____ Wheel Type _____

Country _____ Designer _____

Colors

Overall Color Scheme _____

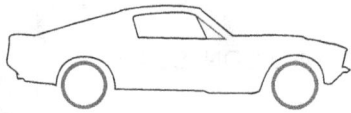

Base _____ Window _____

Fender _____ Interior _____

Where bought? _____

Date Acquired _____

Condition _____

Notes

_____

_____

_____

_____

_____

June

○ 29. MONDAY

PRIORITIES

○ 30. TUESDAY

○ 1. WEDNESDAY

TO DO

○ 2. THURSDAY

○ 3. FRIDAY

○ 4. SATURDAY / 5. SUNDAY

Model Name _____

Collector Number _____   Brand _____

Details

Year _____   Series _____   Wheel Type _____

Country _____   Designer _____

Colors

Overall Color Scheme _____

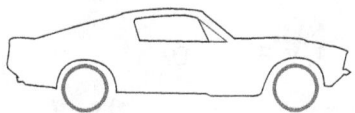

Base _____   Window _____

Fender _____   Interior _____

Where bought? _____

Date Acquired _____

Condition _____

Notes

_____

_____

_____

_____

_____

July

Week 28

○ 6. MONDAY

PRIORITIES

○ 7. TUESDAY

○ 8. WEDNESDAY

TO DO

○ 9. THURSDAY

○ 10. FRIDAY

○ 11. SATURDAY / 12. SUNDAY

Model Name _____

Collector Number _____   Brand _____

Details

Year _____   Series _____   Wheel Type _____

Country _____   Designer _____

Colors

Overall Color Scheme _____

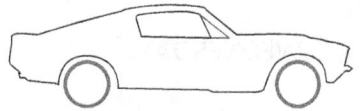

Base _____   Window _____

Fender _____   Interior _____

Notes

Where bought? _____   _____

_____

Date Acquired _____   _____

_____

Condition _____   _____

_____

July

07/13/20 - 07/19/20

○ 13. MONDAY

PRIORITIES

○ 14. TUESDAY

○ 15. WEDNESDAY

TO DO

○ 16. THURSDAY

○ 17. FRIDAY

○ 18. SATURDAY / 19. SUNDAY

Model Name _____

Collector Number _____ Brand _____

Details

Year _____ Series _____ Wheel Type _____

Country _____ Designer _____

Colors

Overall Color Scheme _____

Base _____ Window _____

Fender _____ Interior _____

Notes

Where bought? _____

Date Acquired _____

Condition _____

July

07/20/20 - 07/26/20

○ 20. MONDAY

PRIORITIES

○ 21. TUESDAY

○ 22. WEDNESDAY

TO DO

○ 23. THURSDAY

○ 24. FRIDAY

○ 25. SATURDAY / 26. SUNDAY

Model Name

_____

Collector Number _____ Brand _____

Details

Year _____ Series _____ Wheel Type _____

Country _____ Designer _____

Colors

Overall Color Scheme _____

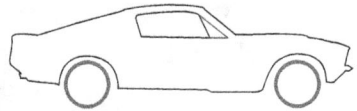

Base _____ Window _____

Fender _____ Interior _____

Where bought? _____

Date Acquired _____

Condition _____

Notes

_____

_____

_____

_____

_____

_____

July

07/27/20 - 08/02/20

○ 27. MONDAY

PRIORITIES

○ 28. TUESDAY

○ 29. WEDNESDAY

TO DO

○ 30. THURSDAY

○ 31. FRIDAY

○ 1. SATURDAY / 2. SUNDAY

Model Name

Collector Number _____   Brand _____

Details

Year _____   Series _____   Wheel Type _____

Country _____   Designer _____

Colors

Overall Color Scheme _____

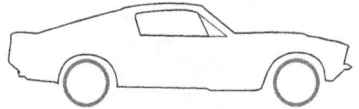

Base _____   Window _____

Fender _____   Interior _____

Notes

Where bought? _____

Date Acquired _____

Condition _____

_____

_____

_____

_____

_____

August

Week 32   08/03/20 - 08/09/20

○ 3. MONDAY

PRIORITIES

○ 4. TUESDAY

○ 5. WEDNESDAY

TO DO

○ 6. THURSDAY

○ 7. FRIDAY

○ 8. SATURDAY / 9. SUNDAY

Model Name _____

Collector Number _____ Brand _____

Details

Year _____ Series _____ Wheel Type _____

Country _____ Designer _____

Colors

Overall Color Scheme _____

Base _____ Window _____

Fender _____ Interior _____

Notes

Where bought? _____ _____

_____

Date Acquired _____ _____

_____

Condition _____ _____

_____

August

08/10/20 - 08/16/20

○ 10. MONDAY

PRIORITIES

_____

_____

○ 11. TUESDAY

_____

_____

_____

○ 12. WEDNESDAY

TO DO

_____

_____

○ 13. THURSDAY

_____

_____

_____

_____

○ 14. FRIDAY

_____

_____

_____

_____

○ 15. SATURDAY / 16. SUNDAY

_____

_____

_____

Model Name _____

Collector Number _____ Brand _____

Details
Year _____ Series _____ Wheel Type _____

Country _____ Designer _____

Colors

Overall Color Scheme _____

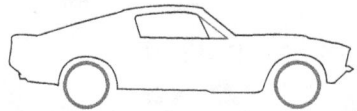

Base _____ Window _____

Fender _____ Interior _____

Where bought? _____

Date Acquired _____

Condition _____

Notes
_____
_____
_____
_____
_____

August

○ 17. MONDAY

PRIORITIES

_____

_____

○ 18. TUESDAY

_____

_____

_____

_____

○ 19. WEDNESDAY

TO DO

_____

_____

○ 20. THURSDAY

_____

_____

_____

_____

○ 21. FRIDAY

_____

_____

_____

_____

○ 22. SATURDAY / 23. SUNDAY

_____

_____

_____

Model Name _____

Collector Number _____ Brand _____

Details

Year _____ Series _____ Wheel Type _____

Country _____ Designer _____

Colors

Overall Color Scheme _____

Base _____ Window _____

Fender _____ Interior _____

Where bought? _____

Date Acquired _____

Condition _____

Notes

_____
_____
_____
_____
_____

August

08/24/20 - 08/30/20

○ 24. MONDAY

PRIORITIES

○ 25. TUESDAY

○ 26. WEDNESDAY

TO DO

○ 27. THURSDAY

○ 28. FRIDAY

○ 29. SATURDAY / 30. SUNDAY

Model Name _____

Collector Number _____ Brand _____

Details

Year _____ Series _____ Wheel Type _____

Country _____ Designer _____

Colors

Overall Color Scheme _____

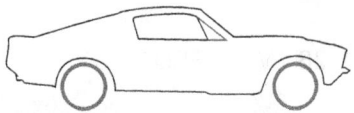

Base _____ Window _____

Fender _____ Interior _____

Notes

Where bought? _____ _____

Date Acquired _____ _____

Condition _____ _____

_____

_____

_____

August

Week 36

08/31/20 - 09/06/20

○ 31. MONDAY

PRIORITIES

○ 1. TUESDAY

○ 2. WEDNESDAY

TO DO

○ 3. THURSDAY

○ 4. FRIDAY

○ 5. SATURDAY / 6. SUNDAY

Model Name

_____

Collector Number _____   Brand _____

Details

Year _____   Series _____   Wheel Type _____

Country _____   Designer _____

Colors

Overall Color Scheme _____

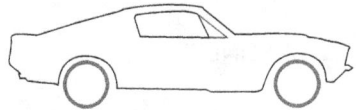

Base _____   Window _____

Fender _____   Interior _____

Notes

Where bought? _____   _____

_____

Date Acquired _____   _____

_____

Condition _____   _____

_____

September

Week 37

○ 7. MONDAY

PRIORITIES

○ 8. TUESDAY

○ 9. WEDNESDAY

TO DO

○ 10. THURSDAY

○ 11. FRIDAY

○ 12. SATURDAY / 13. SUNDAY

Model Name _____

Collector Number _____   Brand _____

Details

Year _____   Series _____   Wheel Type _____

Country _____   Designer _____

Colors

Overall Color Scheme _____

Base _____   Window _____

Fender _____   Interior _____

Where bought? _____

Date Acquired _____

Condition _____

Notes

_____

_____

_____

_____

_____

September

Week 38

09/14/20 - 09/20/20

○ 14. MONDAY

PRIORITIES

○ 15. TUESDAY

○ 16. WEDNESDAY

TO DO

○ 17. THURSDAY

○ 18. FRIDAY

○ 19. SATURDAY / 20. SUNDAY

Model Name _____

Collector Number _____ Brand _____

Details

Year _____ Series _____ Wheel Type _____

Country _____ Designer _____

Colors

Overall Color Scheme _____

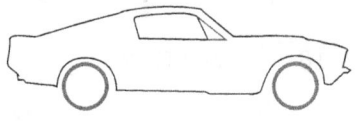

Base _____ Window _____

Fender _____ Interior _____

Notes

Where bought? _____

Date Acquired _____

Condition _____

September

09/21/20 - 09/27/20

○ 21. MONDAY

PRIORITIES

○ 22. TUESDAY

○ 23. WEDNESDAY

TO DO

○ 24. THURSDAY

○ 25. FRIDAY

○ 26. SATURDAY / 27. SUNDAY

Model Name _____

Collector Number _____ Brand _____

Details

Year _____ Series _____ Wheel Type _____

Country _____ Designer _____

Colors

Overall Color Scheme _____

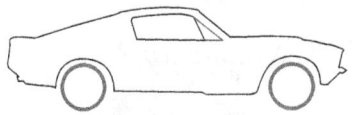

Base _____ Window _____

Fender _____ Interior _____

Notes

Where bought? _____

Date Acquired _____

Condition _____

September

Week 40

09/28/20 - 10/04/20

○ 28. MONDAY

PRIORITIES

○ 29. TUESDAY

○ 30. WEDNESDAY

TO DO

○ 1. THURSDAY

○ 2. FRIDAY

○ 3. SATURDAY / 4. SUNDAY

Model Name

_____

Collector Number _____ Brand _____

Details

Year _____ Series _____ Wheel Type _____

Country _____ Designer _____

Colors

Overall Color Scheme _____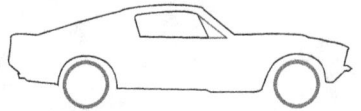

Base _____ Window _____

Fender _____ Interior _____

Notes

Where bought? _____ _____

_____

Date Acquired _____ _____

_____

Condition _____ _____

_____

October

Week 41   10/05/20 - 10/11/20

○ 5. MONDAY

PRIORITIES

○ 6. TUESDAY

○ 7. WEDNESDAY

TO DO

○ 8. THURSDAY

○ 9. FRIDAY

○ 10. SATURDAY / 11. SUNDAY

Model Name _____

Collector Number _____   Brand _____

Details

Year _____   Series _____   Wheel Type _____

Country _____   Designer _____

Colors

Overall Color Scheme _____

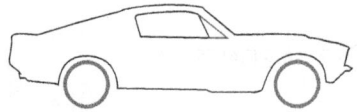

Base _____   Window _____

Fender _____   Interior _____

Where bought? _____

Date Acquired _____

Condition _____

Notes

_____

_____

_____

_____

_____

_____

October

10/12/20 - 10/18/20

○ 12. MONDAY

PRIORITIES

○ 13. TUESDAY

○ 14. WEDNESDAY

TO DO

○ 15. THURSDAY

○ 16. FRIDAY

○ 17. SATURDAY / 18. SUNDAY

Model Name

_____

Collector Number _____ Brand _____

Details

Year _____ Series _____ Wheel Type _____

Country _____ Designer _____

Colors

Overall Color Scheme _____

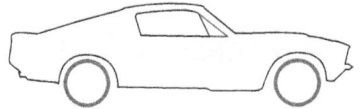

Base _____ Window _____

Fender _____ Interior _____

Where bought? _____

Date Acquired _____

Condition _____

Notes

_____

_____

_____

_____

_____

_____

October

Week 43   10/19/20 - 10/25/20

○ 19. MONDAY

PRIORITIES

○ 20. TUESDAY

○ 21. WEDNESDAY

TO DO

○ 22. THURSDAY

○ 23. FRIDAY

○ 24. SATURDAY / 25. SUNDAY

Model Name _____

Collector Number _____   Brand _____

Details

Year _____   Series _____   Wheel Type _____

Country _____   Designer _____

Colors

Overall Color Scheme _____

Base _____   Window _____

Fender _____   Interior _____

Notes

Where bought? _____   _____

_____

Date Acquired _____   _____

_____

Condition _____   _____

_____

October

10/26/20 - 11/01/20

○ 26. MONDAY

PRIORITIES

_____

_____

○ 27. TUESDAY

_____

_____

_____

_____

○ 28. WEDNESDAY

TO DO

_____

_____

○ 29. THURSDAY

_____

_____

_____

_____

○ 30. FRIDAY

_____

_____

_____

_____

○ 31. SATURDAY / 1. SUNDAY

_____

_____

_____

Model Name _____

Collector Number _____ Brand _____

Details

Year _____ Series _____ Wheel Type _____

Country _____ Designer _____

Colors

Overall Color Scheme _____

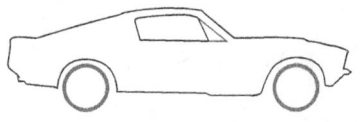

Base _____ Window _____

Fender _____ Interior _____

Where bought? _____

Date Acquired _____

Condition _____

Notes

_____

_____

_____

_____

_____

November

Week 45

11/02/20 - 11/08/20

○ 2. MONDAY

PRIORITIES

○ 3. TUESDAY

○ 4. WEDNESDAY

TO DO

○ 5. THURSDAY

○ 6. FRIDAY

○ 7. SATURDAY / 8. SUNDAY

Model Name _____

Collector Number _____ Brand _____

Details ──────────────────

Year _____ Series _____ Wheel Type _____

Country _____ Designer _____

Colors ──────────────────

Overall Color Scheme _____

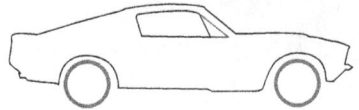

Base _____ Window _____

Fender _____ Interior _____

Where bought? _____

Date Acquired _____

Condition _____

Notes ──────────────────

_____

_____

_____

_____

_____

November

11/09/20 - 11/15/20

○ 9. MONDAY

PRIORITIES

○ 10. TUESDAY

○ 11. WEDNESDAY

TO DO

○ 12. THURSDAY

○ 13. FRIDAY

○ 14. SATURDAY / 15. SUNDAY

Model Name _____

Collector Number _____ Brand _____

Details

Year _____ Series _____ Wheel Type _____

Country _____ Designer _____

Colors

Overall Color Scheme _____

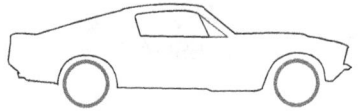

Base _____ Window _____

Fender _____ Interior _____

Notes

Where bought? _____

Date Acquired _____

Condition _____

November

Week 47   11/16/20 - 11/22/20

○ 16. MONDAY

PRIORITIES

_____

_____

○ 17. TUESDAY

_____

_____

_____

_____

○ 18. WEDNESDAY

TO DO

_____

_____

○ 19. THURSDAY

_____

_____

_____

_____

○ 20. FRIDAY

_____

_____

_____

_____

○ 21. SATURDAY / 22. SUNDAY

_____

_____

_____

_____

Model Name

Collector Number _____ Brand _____

Details

Year _____ Series _____ Wheel Type _____

Country _____ Designer _____

Colors

Overall Color Scheme _____

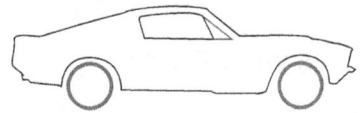

Base _____ Window _____

Fender _____ Interior _____

Notes

Where bought? _____

Date Acquired _____

Condition _____

November

11/23/20 - 11/29/20

○ 23. MONDAY

PRIORITIES

_____

○ 24. TUESDAY

_____

_____

_____

_____

○ 25. WEDNESDAY

TO DO

_____

_____

○ 26. THURSDAY

_____

_____

_____

_____

_____

○ 27. FRIDAY

_____

_____

_____

_____

○ 28. SATURDAY / 29. SUNDAY

_____

_____

_____

Model Name _____

Collector Number _____ Brand _____

Details

Year _____ Series _____ Wheel Type _____

Country _____ Designer _____

Colors

Overall Color Scheme _____

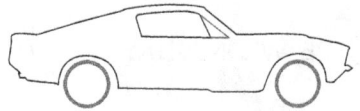

Base _____ Window _____

Fender _____ Interior _____

Notes

Where bought? _____

Date Acquired _____

Condition _____

November

11/30/20 - 12/06/20

○ 30. MONDAY

PRIORITIES

○ 1. TUESDAY

○ 2. WEDNESDAY

TO DO

○ 3. THURSDAY

○ 4. FRIDAY

○ 5. SATURDAY / 6. SUNDAY

Model Name _____

Collector Number _____ Brand _____

Details

Year _____ Series _____ Wheel Type _____

Country _____ Designer _____

Colors

Overall Color Scheme _____

Base _____ Window _____

Fender _____ Interior _____

Where bought? _____

Date Acquired _____

Condition _____

Notes

_____

_____

_____

_____

_____

December

Week 50   12/07/20 - 12/13/20

○ 7. MONDAY

                                                PRIORITIES

○ 8. TUESDAY

○ 9. WEDNESDAY

                                                TO DO

○ 10. THURSDAY

○ 11. FRIDAY

○ 12. SATURDAY / 13. SUNDAY

Model Name _____

Collector Number _____   Brand _____

Details

Year _____   Series _____   Wheel Type _____

Country _____   Designer _____

Colors

Overall Color Scheme _____

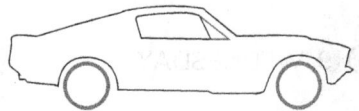

Base _____   Window _____

Fender _____   Interior _____

Where bought? _____

Date Acquired _____

Condition _____

Notes

_____

_____

_____

_____

_____

December

Week 51   12/14/20 - 12/20/20

○ 14. MONDAY

PRIORITIES

○ 15. TUESDAY

○ 16. WEDNESDAY

TO DO

○ 17. THURSDAY

○ 18. FRIDAY

○ 19. SATURDAY / 20. SUNDAY

Model Name

Collector Number _____   Brand _____

Details

Year _____   Series _____   Wheel Type _____

Country _____   Designer _____

Colors

Overall Color Scheme _____

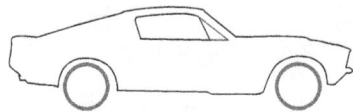

Base _____   Window _____

Fender _____   Interior _____

Where bought? _____

Date Acquired _____

Condition _____

Notes

_____

_____

_____

_____

_____

December

12/21/20 - 12/27/20

○ 21. MONDAY

PRIORITIES

_____

_____

○ 22. TUESDAY

_____

_____

_____

○ 23. WEDNESDAY

TO DO

_____

_____

○ 24. THURSDAY

_____

_____

_____

_____

○ 25. FRIDAY

_____

_____

_____

_____

○ 26. SATURDAY / 27. SUNDAY

_____

_____

_____

Model Name

Collector Number _____ Brand _____

Details

Year _____ Series _____ Wheel Type _____

Country _____ Designer _____

Colors

Overall Color Scheme _____

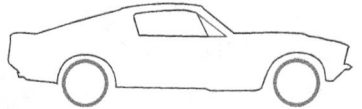

Base _____ Window _____

Fender _____ Interior _____

Notes

Where bought? _____

Date Acquired _____

Condition _____

December

Week 53

12/28/20 - 01/03/21

○ 28. MONDAY

PRIORITIES

○ 29. TUESDAY

○ 30. WEDNESDAY

TO DO

○ 31. THURSDAY

○ 1. FRIDAY

○ 2. SATURDAY / 3. SUNDAY

Weekly Planner 2020

Car Collector

Name:

_____

_____

www.ingramcontent.com/pod-product-compliance
Lightning Source LLC
Chambersburg PA
CBHW060242230326
41458CB00094B/1412